THE CATHEDRAL BUILDERS

THE CATHEDRAL BUILDERS

BY MARIE-PIERRE PERDRIZET

Illustrated by Eddy Krähenbühl
Translated by Mary Beth Raycraft

PEOPLES OF THE PAST

The Millbrook Press
Brookfield, Connecticut

First published in the United States by
The Millbrook Press, Inc.
2 Old New Milford Road, Brookfield
Connecticut 06804

Translation copyright © 1992 by The Millbrook Press

Copyright © 1990 by Editions Nathan, Paris

Originally published as Les bâtisseurs de cathédrales
(Peuples du passé series), Editions Nathan, Paris

Map credit: p. 54—David Prebenna

Library of Congress Cataloging-in-Publication Data

Perdrizet, Marie-Pierre.
[Bâtisseurs de cathédrales. English]
The cathedral builders / by Marie-Pierre Perdrizet and Eddy
Krähenbühl: translated by Mary Beth Raycraft.
p. cm.—(Peoples of the past)
Translation of: Les bâtisseurs de cathédrales.
Includes bibliographical references and index.
Summary: Describes the construction of Gothic cathedrals and
the significance they had in the lives of those who built them.
ISBN 1-56294-162-3
1. Cathedrals—Juvenile literature.   2. Christian art and
symbolism—Medieval, 500–1500—Juvenile literature.
[1. Cathedrals.   2. Civilization, Medieval.]   I. Krähenbühl, Eddy.
II. Title.   III. Series: Peoples of the past (Brookfield, Conn.)
NA4830.P3713   1992
726'.6'0940902—dc20   91-24233 CIP AC

CONTENTS

THE TIME OF THE CATHEDRAL

All through Europe, in villages, towns, and large bustling cities, the spires of cathedrals built in the Middle Ages rise majestically to the skies. In small towns, the cathedral is the longest, widest, and tallest of all the buildings by far. Its tremendous height keeps the sun from shining in the streets and shops around its base. Passersby make their way through the shaded streets as though in the shadow of a giant.

Statues frame the covered entrance to the cathedral, which is capped by a pointed arch. People who pass through its massive doors are dwarfed in comparison. High up, in the center of the building's facade, or front, is a huge circular window made up of different pieces of colored glass.

Inside, it is dark, except for the soft colored light coming through the few windows. People shiver in the sudden chill. Footsteps resound sharply on the flagstones, and the sounds fade away into the silence of the many arches that form the vaulted ceiling.

In Paris these arches are 98 feet (30 meters) high. In other European cities, cathedral arches rise even higher—121 feet (37 meters) in Chartres, 138 (42) in Amiens, 141 (43) in Cologne, and 157 (48) in Beauvais.

The people who built the cathedrals seemed to be competing with one another to enclose as much open space within the cathedral walls as they could, to stretch the imagination by pushing up and still farther up into the air. Above the vaults are towers and spires over 300 feet (92 meters) tall. The spire of Salisbury cathedral in England measures 404 feet (123 meters), as high as a thirty-five story building.

Where Does the Word *Cathedral* Come From?

Cathedral comes from the Latin word cathedra, *the name of the throne on which the bishop sat in his church.*

The Christians in the Middle Ages

The only part of the world recognized by the church in the Middle Ages was Christian Europe. Beyond its borders were pagans and other non-Christians. Most of Africa and Asia were still undiscovered. And, as for America, no one in Europe even knew it existed.

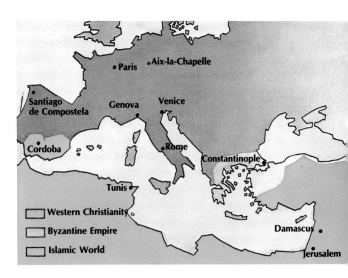

A HOUSE FOR GOD

Today, Gothic cathedrals are from 650 to 850 years old. During the 1100s and 1200s when most of them were planned and constructed, almost everyone in Europe was a Christian. The church was very powerful and played an important part in the daily lives of the people.

If you could ask the people of the Middle Ages why they built the cathedrals—which were very costly undertakings involving thousands of craftsmen and laborers who might spend their entire life toiling at the construction site—they would most likely be surprised that you had asked them.

1. Orvieto

For God, the bishops and monks would have answered. For God and the city, the townspeople would have added.

The cathedral was the house of God. It was also the seat of the bishop, a powerful leader of the church who ruled over an entire region, or diocese, and the clergy, or canons, who served him. A lord had a tower or a castle; a bishop had a cathedral.

This formula no longer applies to European cities. Certain towns that once had a bishop have lost their importance and now seem too small to have such a grand cathedral. Other cities have grown quickly in recent years and do not possess a cathedral.

The presence of a cathedral is no longer the symbol of earthly power and religious faith that it once was.

Today, we enter the huge spaces inside the cathedrals in hushed wonder, but in medieval times (the Middle Ages) the cathedral was woven into the life of the town. It was the house of God, but it was the house of the people too.

Its bells warned the citizens of fire or danger and called the merchants together to discuss the affairs of the town. Every Sunday the bells rang to alert the townspeople and the people who worked in the surrounding fields that it was time to stop their work or play and hurry to the cathedral to hear the bishop say Mass. On the religious holidays sprinkled throughout the year—Easter, Christmas, Pentecost, and saints' days—processions began or ended inside, and the milling crowd spilled out onto its plaza and walkways.

Cathedrals were noisy, crowded places. They were the central meeting point in town. Young people and men and women of all ages met in the aisles to play games, gossip, or engage in heated political discussions. Children gathered around their teacher to do their lessons; travelers stopped in to rest and have a bite to eat; homeless

Cathedral in Reims, France

2. Paris

3. Cologne

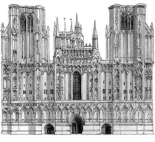

4. Wells

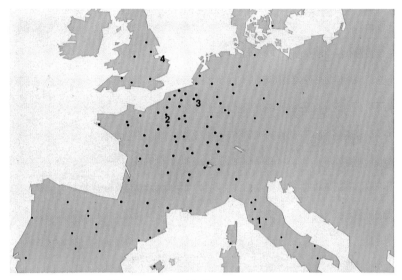

The Cathedrals of Europe in the 1200s

A Cathedral— A Sign of Good Times

Whenever times were good—when the peasants brought in plentiful crops so that shopkeepers grew wealthy selling food to the townspeople, and the news of abundance attracted people from neighboring towns and drew laborers to work in the fields— plans for a cathedral were bound to be under way. The merchants had extra money to contribute for building materials; the church encouraged its followers to support the project; craftsmen and builders flocked to the work site. The cathedral was a symbol of the glory of God and of the wealth of the town. It was a sign of both economic prosperity and faith.

people curled up and slept there; animals wandered freely in and out; merchants sold their wares on the cathedral steps.

Babies were baptized in the cathedral, and young couples took their wedding vows there. And when people died, they were buried in the sacred grounds of the church cemetery.

Cathedrals set the rhythm of the days and gave meaning to the life and death of the people who built them.

THE TIME WAS RIGHT

Before the time of the Gothic cathedrals, kings and the most powerful lords oversaw the building of their castles, forts, and dungeons. Monks and bishops directed the construction of monasteries, basilicas (large churches), and Roman cathedrals. The lords and the clergy hired specialized artisans, or craftsmen, gathered the necessary money, and relied on the strength of the laborers, many of whom were peasants. These peasants had no choice but to work, and often without pay, because they were in servitude to their masters, the lords and wealthy landowners.

The power and resources necessary to direct the construction of the cathedrals in the 1100s and 1200s were even greater. It was not until this time of relative peace and prosperity that cathedrals were able to come into being. Europe was free from invaders, and people settled down to cultivate the land.

Peasants produced an abundance of crops where the soil was rich and the fields were well cultivated. There was a great coming and going between the country and the town as wagons piled high with goods headed from the farmland to the marketplace and back again.

Château Gaillard

Gisors

Beaumaris Castle

Castles

At the same time that cathedrals were under construction, the kings continued to have fortresses, towers, and city ramparts, or walls, constructed. The most skilled masons and stone and wood "engineers" worked for the king.

In less than two years, Richard the Lionhearted (Richard Coeur de Lion), the king of England, established Château Gaillard in Normandy to hold off his enemy Philip Augustus, in 1196. At the same time, Philip Augustus constructed dungeons in Dourdan, Gisors, Lillebonne, and Rouen.

At Beaumaris Castle in England, the king employed more than 1,500 workers at one time, in 1278.

Carcassonne

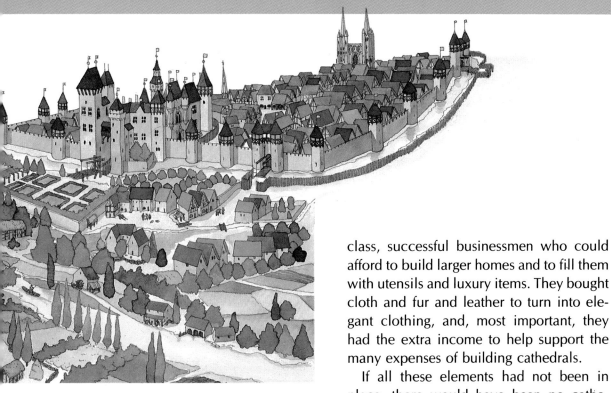

From the vines and pastures came wine and meat for the shops. From the fields and gardens came grains and vegetables. On market days, masses of villagers streamed into the cities alongside the cartloads of produce. People and ideas circulated. Technical advances were shared.

Masons and carpenters moved into the growing cities to build housing for the newcomers who were settling on the outskirts of town. In many regions at this time, the number of dwellers doubled during a single century. Artisans and shopkeepers opened new stores or expanded their old ones.

A class of people began to emerge, called the bourgeoisie. They formed the first middle class, successful businessmen who could afford to build larger homes and to fill them with utensils and luxury items. They bought cloth and fur and leather to turn into elegant clothing, and, most important, they had the extra income to help support the many expenses of building cathedrals.

If all these elements had not been in place, there would have been no cathedrals. And in certain isolated regions, where the climate was less favorable, the soil was poor, and trade did not increase, the towns remained small. There, even if people had imagined the possibility of building such a grand monument, in reality the dream did not take hold.

BASILICAS, BAPTISTRIES, CHURCHES, AND ABBEYS

Long before Christians began to build Gothic cathedrals, people gathered together in other kinds of buildings. Most of these were built after the year 1000. By the year 1300, the church had built around 300,000 places of worship of many different sizes all over Europe. Several hundred of these religious buildings were so vast that they could hold the entire population of a village.

Basilicas were the first large religious buildings. They were modeled after Roman meeting rooms of the same name.

A medieval basilica

Baptistry in Parma, Italy

Baptistries are places where new believers are welcomed into the Christian faith. On the day of their baptism, they are sprinkled with water from a font, or basin.

Hermitages, oratories, and chapels are small places of worship. In the first centuries A.D., they were often made of the same rough stones, wood, or clay used for the village houses of the time. They show that Christianity spread into rural areas.

Church of Saint Pierre in Brancion, France

Parish churches: From the 1100s on, almost every village built its own church, and every city constructed its own neighborhood, or parish, churches.

Abbeys: Monks erected monasteries in even the most isolated of places. Those run by a father abbot were called abbeys. They contained dormitories, a dining hall, workshops, and other buildings, as well as a church.

Oratory of Gallarus Dingle, Ireland

Cloister of the Fontenay abbey, France

THE COSTS OF CONSTRUCTION

To build a monument as massive and complex as a cathedral required powerful leadership, many workers, an enormous quantity of stone, skilled builders capable of applying the latest techniques, and, above all, lots of money.

Some of this money came from the clergy and the noblemen. Other funds came from the growing number of bourgeois (middle-class) merchants who had accumulated their wealth by trading the fruits of the harvests and the many items created by the skilled craftsmen.

Each year the clergy of the cathedral in Autun did their books. Aside from paying the workers' salaries and buying the stone and wood for the construction, they had many other expenses to account for: the lime for the mortar; the nails and metal pieces; the carts; the roofing boards; the master builder's living expenses; his new outfit; hammers for the roofers; saddles, bridles, and reins for the oxen and carts; straw and hay for the horses; the needs of sick animals; and so on.

It was difficult to meet all these expenses over the many decades, or perhaps a century or more, of a cathedral's construction.

After using up their own reserves and those of the bishops, the members of the chapter, the very wealthy religious body in charge of the construction, had to rely on their imagination.

When the project first got under way, the townspeople were very generous. The bishop delivered a moving sermon, creating enthusiasm throughout the city. The people offered what they could for the construction. The canons and bishop set an example by donating some of their income. As time went on, though, expenses increased and the excitement began to wear off. All year long, monks asked for donations in the squares of the churches and in front of the construction site. They put collection boxes inside the places of worship and in the shops and houses of the most well known

craftsmen of the town. Along with the church, it was the king, the princes and lords of the region, and the successful tradespeople who were able to give the most.

The End of an Era

In 14th-century France, the influential center of Gothic architecture, enthusiasm for building was lacking. Difficulties brought on by the war with the English, the plague, and economic hardship broke the spirit of the workers.

As they lay dying, lords and merchants willed their earthly goods to the cathedral. They did this because they were religious and also because they wanted the protection of the Virgin Mary or a saint so that they might enter paradise. These richest members of the bourgeoisie hoped that they would be pardoned for having earned so much money on earth. The priests had told them over and over that making a profit was not worthy of a Christian.

Sometimes, despite these enormous efforts, there would still be no money to continue the project. The men of the church would then look for other ways to fund the construction. The monks would take advantage of market days, fairs, and religious

Tomb of Eleanor of Aquitaine

holidays to call on the generosity of the townspeople, or laymen, or they would travel to neighboring areas requesting money. People would give what money they could or offer food and drink to the desperate workers.

Often, work would start up again after a while, but sometimes the construction site closed down for good. It was simply beyond the means of the people to finish their cathedral. They would decide to use their donations to build a home for the sick and the poor or to rebuild an old monastery at the outskirts of town.

HOW LONG IT TOOK
TO BUILD THEM

Today, a construction site is always surrounded by a fence. Hydraulic shovels and bulldozers compete with jackhammers in a large open space. Any remaining parts of a previous structure are torn down. The cranes are ready to unload panels that have already been constructed at a factory. If the plans and financing are in order, a new opera house or a modern museum will be completed within a few months or, at most, a few years.

In the time of the cathedrals, the work progressed at a much slower pace. In 1220, the bishop of Amiens laid the first stone of his cathedral. By 1269, the last windows were in place. It took about fifty years to finish construction. The cathedral in Chartres took more than thirty-five years to build. It took sixty-five years to complete Laon, eighty for Bourges, and more than one hundred for the Senlis cathedral. Throughout the 1100s and 1200s, many cathedrals were nothing more than an enormous construction site.

The rhythm of work was set by the tread of oxen bringing materials and the men digging the earth with their shovels. And yet, it was a lively scene. While laborers knocked down the crumbling walls of an old church, others took apart the houses that were too close by, or pushed back the walls of the city. Carts as wide as the streets lumbered by, sagging under the weight of the first stones. Some workers dug the foundations; others unloaded the enormous blocks. The townspeople looked on as the masons started to put up the first wall. Many of these people would not live long enough to see their cathedral finished.

Although medieval builders had much experience in the construction of many other kinds of buildings, none of them—dungeons, miles of walls around cities, fortresses, the arches supporting bridges—was as tall, vast, or slender as the Gothic cathedral. Nor did any equal its perfection of form and technical complexity.

Who Built the People's Houses?

The people of the Middle Ages always built their own homes. They used whatever natural materials they could find around them: wood for the posts and beams, clay to make walls of dried mud, and bundles of reeds for the roof. Those who lived in the great forests of the east built huts out of logs. In southern Europe, small stone houses, made with neither cement nor mortar, were often covered with tiles.

BUILDING THE CATHEDRAL

Around the year 1200, there were a number of reasons for building a cathedral. To begin with, the region had to be flourishing to plan this monumental thanks to God for his bounty. Yet there were other considerations as well. An old Roman cathedral may have burned to the ground. A church may have become too small to handle the growing number of its worshipers. Or, a bishop may have seen a wonderful cathedral in a neighboring town and, backed by the church and the bourgeoisie, collected the funds to replace his old cathedral with a new, more beautiful one.

Once the decision was made, a council would meet. The bishop, a person as important as a lord or a prince, was there, as were the wealthiest bourgeois of the town. But it was the canons, a special group of clergymen, also known as clerics, who were in charge of the project. Together, they formed what was called the cathedral's *chapter*. This chapter decided where the cathedral would be built, and it hired and paid the salaries of the workers.

THE MASTER BUILDER

"In the year 1220, work on this church began. The bishop of the diocese was Evrard and the King of France was Louis, son of Philip the Wise. The director of the project was master Robert de Luzarches. Thomas de Cormont took over after him, and then came his son Renaud who had this record inscribed . . ."

This rare inscription was carved on a stone slab long ago in the Amiens cathedral. It says that three masters worked on the ca-

thedral. The workers who made the plans and directed the construction were not called architects. They were called masters or master builders. It was Renaud, the last master, who tells us who the three masters of the Amiens cathedral were.

One master's tombstone bears the inscription "doctor of stone." Another builder was described as "an energetic man, an ingenious stone and wood worker." More often, however, the names of the masters have been forgotten. It was not until the 1200s that people began to respect the talent, ability, and daring of these men.

These were the men who drew the plans and supervised the construction. Perhaps the town would have heard of a master who had created a beautiful cathedral in a neighboring town, and they would ask him

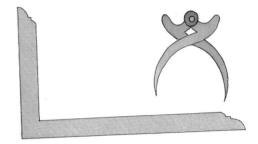

A Master Builder's Tomb

Hue Libergie lived in the 1200s. In his right hand he holds a church, perhaps a model of one he himself built. In his left hand he holds a measuring stick. At his feet are dividers and a square for drawing plans.

to draw up a plan for them. Or, a man might simply convince the bishop and priests of the cathedral that his plans would produce a cathedral to surpass all others.

This man might be a cleric, or perhaps a monk who had studied a bit of mathematics, or a mason or carpenter who had learned the art of building and making plans at a former construction site. The tools of his trade were a measuring stick, a square to figure right angles, and dividers, two pointed sticks hinged together at one end, which allowed him to draw circles.

He presented his plan before the chapter. The builder would trace lines on a plaster board to show his floor plan. He might use a rope to give the canons a sense of the height or unroll a parchment scroll on which he had drawn up his unusual design in greater detail.

If the chapter approved the project, he would run the construction site for a year

or two, or maybe for the rest of his life. These outstanding masters were the first true architects.

THE MEN WHO WORKED AT THE SITE

At the construction site there were two basic groups of workers. In the first group were the master craftsmen. Some were skilled in working with stone: the master quarryman who directed the excavation of huge rocks from a hole in the earth, the master stonecutter who knew how to chisel and hammer the stones into the proper dimensions to use for the walls and columns and arches, and the master sculptor who carved the designs in the stones that would lace the archways, cornices, and columns, or piers. The sculptors also created the statues that would later be placed around the interior chapels and in niches on the outside walls of the cathedral when all was finished.

And then there were the master mortar maker, the master carpenter, the master blacksmith, the master roofer, and the master glassmaker, who supervised the cutting and painting of the colored glass for the windows. All of these experienced craftsmen were assisted by apprentices and assistants who were learning the trade, young men and boys who hoped to become masters themselves one day.

The other large group of men were the manual laborers. They relied on the strength of their back and arms and legs rather than on knowledge of a particular trade. They were hired to work for a day or for a season.

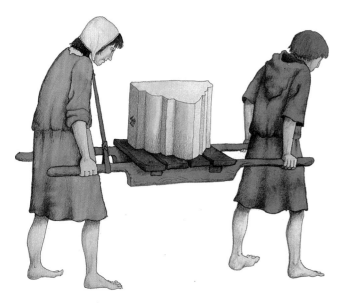

Why Did Blacksmiths Work at the Construction Site?

Medieval builders needed blacksmiths to forge the iron tools that were used to cut and sculpt the stones for the cathedral walls and arches and to make the tongs used to lift these heavy stones. Blacksmiths made all the other tools needed for construction as well—nails, braces to reinforce the walls, and shoes for the oxen and horses that pulled the wagons to the work site. The most talented of the blacksmiths even made locks, bolts, and iron fences.

Some workers, called pieceworkers, were even paid by the job for each stone or molding they cut.

Dozens of workers were hired to clear the ground, dig the foundations, put up the scaffolding, and hoist the stones and containers of mortar. All day long, they broke the ground with pickaxes and dug the earth up with wooden shovels reinforced with

iron. Some carried the dirt away in large baskets. Assistants carried the water, sand, and limestone to the workplace in buckets. The master mortar maker stirred these together in a shallow wooden container called a trough. The mixture was used to hold stones together and to coat the walls and vaults, or arched ceilings, of the cathedrals.

Still others, called loaders, transported building materials from one end of the construction site to another. Wheelbarrows, so practical for carrying heavy loads, were not in use at this time.

In spring and summer, all these workers toiled together to clear the site and lay the foundation stones. Very gradually, the walls would begin to rise. The men worked at the site from sunrise to sunset. In the middle of the day, they went to the temporary huts built at the foot of the cathedral to eat bread and drink wine. At night, some of the workers slept at the site. Others returned to their homes or to rented rooms in town.

With the coming of winter, activity at the site slowed down. The only workers to stay on were the sculptors, who continued to carve the stone. The masons and mortar makers stopped working because the mortar might freeze when the temperature dropped. They protected the unfinished walls by covering them with straw and then went to their homes. The manual laborers, too, were out of work.

Theirs was a tough life. They had to survive the long winter months without any pay, and even during the working months, it was hard to make ends meet. The master craftsmen were the highest-paid workers. They were often given housing, food, and clothing in addition to their salary. The manual laborers were paid least of all. The lowest paid among them were the piece-workers, peasants who had recently arrived in the village. They were rarely hired for more than five days a week, whereas the other workers averaged a six-day week.

Religious holidays were frequent. In addition to the fifty-two Sundays of the year, there were forty feast days. On those days, the workers had to get by without receiving any pay.

Some workers were not paid at all. These were peasants who owed favors to their master. Instead of repaying him by working at his castle or on his land, they were ordered to use their oxen and carts to transport materials from the neighboring towns to the cathedral.

Sometimes monks, pilgrims, or devoted members of the community volunteered to work on the cathedral, but often the workers, who were anxious to keep their jobs, looked on these outsiders with mistrust. A novel was written in 12th-century France that illustrates the seriousness of their suspicions.

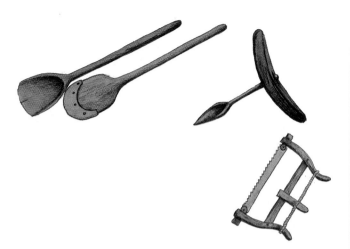

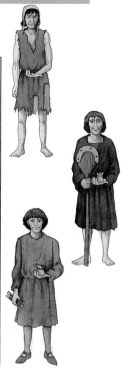

The hero, Renaut de Montauban, wishes to be pardoned for his wrongdoings. He volunteers as a manual laborer at a cathedral's construction site. There, from morning till night, he carries the heaviest stones and lifts buckets filled with mortar. But the workers distrust this man who works so hard for only a little bit of bread. One day, they kill him with a blow on the head and throw him into the river.

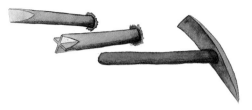

THE STONES OF THE CATHEDRAL

Medieval builders cut, transported, and arranged several million tons of stone. Reinforced concrete had not yet been invented, and iron construction was beyond imagining at the time. Stone was the strongest and best material available in large quantities.

It was excavated, or dug out of the ground, at a quarry, a big hole located as near to the construction site as possible. Sometimes particularly beautiful stones were taken from the ruins of buildings.

During the years of the cathedral's construction, the quarry hummed with the sound of iron picks, chisels, hammers, and massive wooden machines in motion. There was even a workshop and a forge where the blacksmiths made and repaired the tools used in excavating and shaping the stones.

The master quarryman supervised dozens of stonecutters and hundreds of laborers. The workers detached the rock from the earth by inserting wooden wedges into the stones and pounding the wedges with mallets until they split. Thick hemp ropes suspended from pulleys were looped around the stone. Little by little the blocks were inched up from the quarry by means of enormous winches and moved away from the hole. These simple machines made it possible for a single man to lift 1,340 pounds (608 kilograms) of stone.

Often, stonecutters would start to chip up the blocks right at the quarry to avoid transporting extra weight to the construction site. They shaped the stones to the specifications of the master mason. Since the cutters were paid by the stone, they chiseled their individual mark in each one when they were finished. Two additional marks were made: one to identify the quarry

the stone came from and another to show where it should be placed in the cathedral. It is still possible to see the stonecutters' marks on the walls of medieval buildings.

After the stones were prepared at the quarry, workers used a cart pulled by oxen to move them to the construction site. It took them half a day to go only 9 miles (15 kilometers). The heavy cargo made deep ruts in the earth, and sometimes the stones

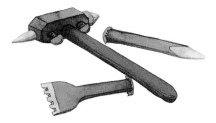

tumbled off the carts into the ditches at the side of the road.

In the winter, when the peasants had no work in the fields, they were hired to carry loads in their carts back and forth between the quarry and the construction site. However, if there was a river nearby, this natural pathway was used instead. In Amiens, for instance, cargo boats transported stones along the Somme River. The Norwich cathedral in England was built with creamy gold stones from Caen, a city to the west of Paris, that came across the English Channel in a boat.

Muscle Power

A man could carry as much as 65 pounds (30 kilograms) on his back. Mules could transport approximately 400 pounds (182 kilograms) in their packsaddles. Several oxen hitched to a wagon could pull 3,000 to 8,000 pounds (1,350 to 3,600 kilograms) in a single load.

RAISING THE WALLS

With the birth of the Gothic cathedral, walls scaled incredible heights. They were built to last. The walls had to stand straight and bear the tremendous load of the arches and the massive vaulted ceilings. This demanded careful planning, technical knowledge, and skilled craftsmen.

Medieval masons knew that their walls would not hold unless they were firmly secured in the ground. This is why construction always began with an enormous hole. After digging and preparing the necessary foundations, the masons worked quickly for as long as their supplies held out.

A wall was not simply a bunch of stones piled on top of one another. The stones for a cathedral were chosen and sculpted one by one. The master mason planned everything in advance down to the dimensions of each stone and the way in which the stones would be stacked. Assistants rolled the largest blocks from the carts on logs and dragged them on stretchers, while they carried the smallest ones in baskets.

The craftsmen placed each shaped stone on a layer of mortar and pressed it down by striking it with a mallet. A layer of mortar was smoothed on between each stone and each of the new layers with trowels.

The master scurried around to check carefully with his level and plumb line to ensure that each new layer was perfectly in line. If the wall began to dip or bulge out on top, or if it leaned in or out, the builders were in trouble. If they had not

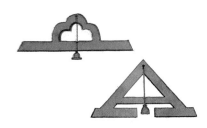

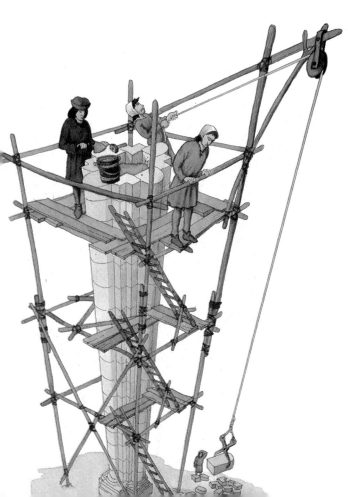

been so careful, these walls would never be standing today.

Meanwhile, others were working continuously to prepare the mortar. If you mix sand with water to build a castle, when it dries, it will crumble. If the mixture is to

More About Stones

A wall is made of two rows of stone. The visible sides are called facings. The space between the rows is filled with small stones and mortar—the concrete of the Middle Ages.

hold together, you have to add a binder, such as cement. In the Middle Ages, the builders used lime to bind their mortar.

Crushed limestone and wood charcoal were piled in a clay oven. After a long period of baking, the residue, from which all the ashes had been scraped off, was ready to be mixed with water and sand sifted from the riverbanks. By drying slowly, a good mortar binds stones together as well as cement would. But if it freezes, it won't hold. This is why the masons and mortar makers had to stop their work in the winter.

As the walls rose up, the masons had to use wooden ladders and scaffolding to work

on top of them. When they had to climb as high as 100 feet (30 meters), the situation grew more complex. Some masons perched on scaffolds suspended from the framework. Others worked on simple boards placed over horizontal beams that were inserted into the wall for this purpose. Today, you can still see the holes left by these beams in the walls of cathedrals and castles. They are called pigeonholes.

THE GOTHIC VAULT

Embedding the stones in the arches of the vault required an acrobatic mason. Work-related accidents were not uncommon. It's easy to understand why the craftsmen celebrated the completion of important stages of construction, such as the placement of a vault's keystone, an enormous block of stone weighing more than 1,000 pounds (450 kilograms) that closes the gap between the arches of the vault.

In the time of the cathedrals, there was no technological revolution. But there were some new methods in construction that were perfected and passed quickly from one construction site to another.

The major problem the workers faced was how to cover the space between the walls. The first stone vaults spanned only a few yards. Eventually, though, arches were formed by placing blunt, wedge-shaped stones called voussoirs on a framework. But what a weight! In order to support them the workers put up thick walls, pierced with only a few windows.

For the spacious and soaring Gothic cathedrals, the workers created lighter-weight

How to Build a Gothic Vault

Medieval builders left no written instructions on how they built their vaults, and they didn't build them all in the same way. Here's one way they did it:

1. Place the wooden arches on pillars.

2. Construct the arches and the intersecting ribbed vaults.

3. Fill in all the vaults at the same time.

vaults, called ribbed vaults, which rose to a point. Inside, it took only slender columns, or piers, to support them.

When there were several parallel vaults, naves, or aisles, they had to be supported from the outside as well. This was the purpose served by flying buttresses. Without them, the walls would begin to lean outward from the pressure of the vaults, and eventually the cathedral would collapse. If you were to climb onto a cathedral's roof and peer down,

Notre Dame of Paris

The Advantages of This New Technique

1. The height could increase in proportion to the width.
2. The interior pillars could be lighter and more refined.
3. Fewer walls let in more light.

The Choir of Gloucester Cathedral

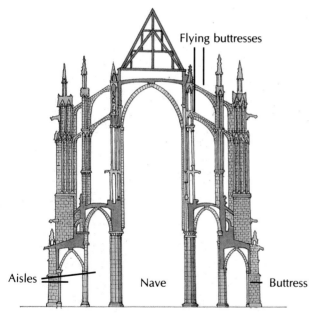

Flying buttresses

Aisles   Nave   Buttress

you'd see a forest of arches surrounding the building. It looks as though the builders left a gigantic framework to support their creation. And in fact, this is exactly what they did.

THE IMPORTANCE OF WOOD

At first glance, there seems to be little or no wood in cathedrals. However, wood played an essential role in supporting the roof, which shelters the stone vaults from the rain.

Until the end of the 12th century, towers, castles, and bridges were usually made of wood. However, in the heavily populated regions of western Europe there was a lot of construction and lumbering of forests to enlarge the increasing fields. In addition, many destructive fires swept through neighborhoods and churches. A serious shortage of wood developed around the year 1200.

Carpenters had to comb the woods of outlying regions and even send to foreign lands for the wood they needed. Sometimes they had to go all the way to Scandinavia to find beams thick and long enough to support the walls of their cathedrals.

Carpenters were involved from the beginning of the project until its end. As soon as the masons finished the walls, the carpenters installed a covering framework of wood. This was immediately protected from the weather by laying sheets of lead, slate,

Roofs

The roofs of houses were often made of limestone. Roofers used lead, slate, or tile for castle towers, cathedrals, and large houses. These materials were much lighter than the tiles used by the Romans or the stones used in mountain areas. Roofers added gutters to cathedral roofs to draw rainwater away from the walls, and stone spouts called "gargoyles" that were carved to look like monsters who spit water when it rained.

or tile for the roof on top of this framework. The masons were then able to erect the vaults within the umbrella of a roof.

The carpenters also made struts, or lengths of wood, that supported the walls while they were being built, and they made scaffolding from young trees. These were more solid than the squared beams of the same width; they neither bent nor splintered. The workers climbed them or made perches on the natural forks of their branches.

And without the scaffolding and the supporting framework for the arches and walls under construction, without the many wooden machines used to lift the stones— the cranes, levers, and great wheels—the construction of the cathedral would not have been possible.

The carpenters were also responsible for a clever contraption called a collapsible arch or a centering. These were used for

supporting the stones of the arches while they were under construction and while the mortar was drying. Beginning around 1200, these centerings were made to be collapsed and reused for the next arches. In this way, the carpenters saved a tremendous amount of wood.

IMAGES IN GLASS AND STONE

The windows of the cathedrals were filled with colored glass. They were carefully placed to create a spectacular effect upon the worshipers as they entered. Colored light poured through the complex patterns of the panes so that visitors had the impression of being encased in precious jewels—sapphire blue, ruby red, and emerald green. In medieval times the effect was even more marvelous than it may seem to us today, because in most buildings of that time wooden shutters or tanned animal hides blocked light passing through windows.

In the words of Guillaume Durand, a man who lived in the 1200s, "stained glass . . . brings the light of the true sun, mean-

How Glass Was Made in the 1100s

Sand and ash were mixed together and then melted over a very hot wood fire. At first, the molten, or melted, mixture turned a greenish color, but artisans added metal dyes to turn it different colors. Next the glassmakers formed a large ball of molten glass at the end of a hollow rod and blew air into it until the glass stretched out like a balloon. Then they cut it, flattened it, or spun it to spread out like a pancake.

The resulting glass was thick, its surface splotched with pits and bumps from air bubbles. Glassmakers knew how to use the imperfections to add to the beauty of their designs.

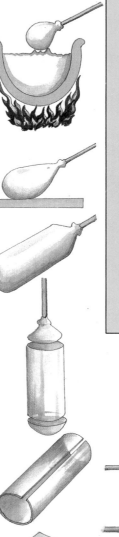

Unknown Artists

Most artists who made stained-glass windows are unknown today, although Clement of Chartres signed a window in the Rousen cathedral. Another glass painter named Gerlachus painted himself holding a paintbrush in one of his windows.

ing God, to the faithful ones in the church by illuminating them.'' The cathedral was a house of worship, and when people entered they were bathed in a special glow symbolic of God's presence on earth.

MAKING THE GLASS

The long and difficult process of glassmaking took place at the edge of the forest. In town, near the construction site, the glass painters cut, assembled, and painted the glass.

On a worktable, a worker traced the pattern for the window in chalk. He was then able to lay the glass over the design and trace the pattern onto the glass. With a sharply pointed rod called a grozing iron, he then cut the glass into many different shapes. He cut the pieces in such a way that, when reassembled, they would be just the right size to fill the space of the window.

The master painted the details of the faces and clothing in black. The painted pieces were put into the oven once more to set the colors in the glass. During this time, an assistant prepared the lead, which would be used to assemble all of the pieces into a mosaic—a complete picture. Finally, the entire window, sometimes up to 60 feet (18 meters) tall, was ready to be hoisted up and put into its place in the cathedral.

Winegrower

Baker

THE WINDOWS TELL STORIES

These delicate, precious windows were expensive to produce. Often, groups of merchants and craftsmen donated the money for their construction. A group, or association, of artisans funded many of the stained glass windows in the cathedral of Chartres, for instance. The most beautiful window was dedicated to these men and placed in the nicest spot in the cathedral.

Each of the panes in this window recalls the life of a saint or a scene from the Bible. But, in the lowest corner, the most visible one, the artisans included pictures of themselves with their tools. In Paris, in 1260, more than a hundred different trades were represented—sculptors, stonecutters, masons, mortar makers, plasterers, carpenters, and blacksmiths. Even bakers, merchants, weavers, and farmers were pictured.

These were the people of the cities and villages who worked on the cathedrals. And as their associations grew more powerful, they were often those who financed them. Even though they filled the colored glass with biblical scenes, they did not hesitate to leave us a more earthly story as well—of those who spent their lives working to create them.

From the windows of Chartres

Bread carriers

Carpenters

Gunsmiths

Money changers

Weavers

Fur merchants

A POPULATION IN STONE

Outside the cathedral, a whole population of stone figures decorate its facades and entranceways. The cathedral of Notre Dame in Paris has 1,200 such statues. At Reims, you can count as many as 3,000 of them.

The most talented and experienced stonecutters made them. They were called image makers because they sculpted images in stone. They used the same tools as the stonecutters: a wooden mallet and a chisel. But for the more delicate work, they used an awl, something like an ice pick, and a chisel. Although they, like the other workers, followed the directions handed down by the bishop, the monks, and the master builder, this didn't stop them from inventing new shapes, perfecting their craft, or creating distinctive masterpieces.

At the work site, the sculptors perched on scaffolding when they carved a row of statues in the wall. But often they preferred to finish their work at the foot of the cathedral before putting it in place. In the extreme temperatures of summer and winter, they took shelter under canopies or wooden huts made specially for them.

A stone worker could cut a stone block within several hours or a large cornice, or molding, in a few days. It took more than a month to carve the long archways of the

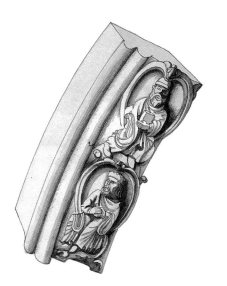

porticos, the covered entrances to a cathedral. But it took the sculptor more than three months to create a single statue.

The time the sculptor spent depended on his ability as well as the hardness of the stone he was carving. Limestone, for example, is much softer than sandstone or granite, and it was frequently used for that reason.

If the sculptor was carving a king or a bishop for the first time, he followed the design traced by his master. If he had experience creating angels or devils, the apostles or the Virgin Mary, he didn't need a model. But he always respected tradition: Christ had bare feet, Mary looked kind, Saint Peter carried the keys to paradise, Saint Michael wore a sword. He did this so that people would have no trouble recognizing the characters. It was important to the sculptor, as well as to the glassmaker, that the population understand the meaning of his work.

WHY THE CATHEDRAL WAS BUILT

The Gothic cathedral served many purposes for the medieval world. It was built to astound those who rounded a distant turn in a road and glimpsed for the first time its majestic spires pointing to the heavens. And it was built to inspire the peasants and townspeople as they toiled at their daily tasks. The cathedral was built to impress those who saw it from afar and those who entered its massive doorways, to be surrounded by the dazzling colored light shining through its stained glass windows.

Most of all, though, the cathedral was built to remind the people of God. In medieval times, it was the church, alongside the king, that organized and ruled over society. The works of art, the craftsmanship, the livelihoods, and even the identities of medieval people were wrapped up in the powerful presence of the church.

"Beautiful God" (Amiens)

The cathedral was the center of the church, and it was in the cathedral that its regulations and traditions were preserved. Mass was held here, the major turning points in life were recognized here, and religious celebrations and holidays took place here.

Not least of all, the cathedral was a teacher for those who knew how to receive its instruction. Like a gigantic book, the cathedral tells the story of medieval people—how they spent their lives, what they knew about the world, what their religious beliefs

A Book With No Words

In the Middle Ages, few people knew how to read and write. Few of them ever even held a book in their hands. Books —made out of specially treated skins known as parchments cut and sewn together—were very rare and expensive. Because the printing press had not yet been invented, monks who worked as copiers wrote every word by hand. For those who would never own a book, the cathedral had images sculpted in stone, stories told in glass, and paintings etched onto enamel and precious materials.

The Devil (Notre Dame in Paris)

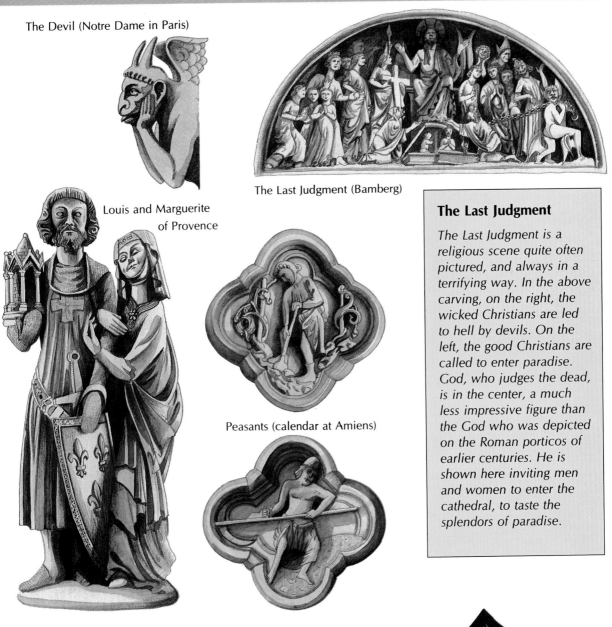

The Last Judgment (Bamberg)

Louis and Marguerite of Provence

Peasants (calendar at Amiens)

The Last Judgment

The Last Judgment is a religious scene quite often pictured, and always in a terrifying way. In the above carving, on the right, the wicked Christians are led to hell by devils. On the left, the good Christians are called to enter paradise. God, who judges the dead, is in the center, a much less impressive figure than the God who was depicted on the Roman porticos of earlier centuries. He is shown here inviting men and women to enter the cathedral, to taste the splendors of paradise.

and traditions were, and how they felt about God.

All this information is built into the very structure of the cathedral—the windows and statues, the carvings in its piers and cornices and archways—and also into the furniture and ornaments and religious objects. All of these taught medieval people, and teach us today, about who they were.

Two knights (Chartres)

The knowledgeable and literate people of the 1200s wrote books about the abundance in the world, scientific discovery, and the history of mankind. The cathedral builders recreated almost all of this knowledge on stained glass and in stone for everyone to see.

The whole world is pictured in the order that the church saw as appropriate. On the sides of the cathedral are important figures from the Bible, such as the prophets and the apostles. On the portico, Christ and the Virgin Mary are surrounded by saints. Farther on are statues of the kings of France and statues that symbolize medicine, ge-

showing religious scenes. There were many religious objects, such as special gold or copper boxes, called tabernacles, and reliquaries (special containers) decorated in enamel or precious stone, which were placed at the altar.

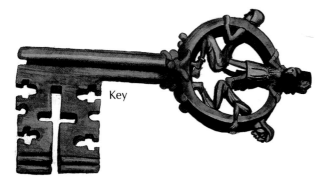

Key

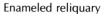

Enameled reliquary

ometry, philosophy, music, painting, and agriculture. Sometimes all of these characters are lined up like the objects of a collector; other times they create scenes from religious history or portray episodes from the life of a saint.

All those who lived during the construction of the cathedrals have their place here as well—members of the clergy, knights in armor, peasants working the land, shopkeepers with their bags of merchandise, bankers and their gold, and even beggars with their hands held out for mercy.

Even the interior decorations, the embroidered tapestries that served as partitions, and the furniture—including the monks' stalls, the bishop's throne, the chests, and the armoires—were masterpieces

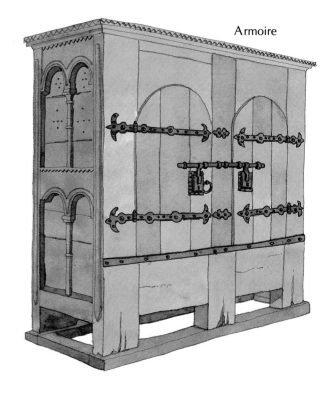

Armoire

Gilded copper ciborium,
or goblet

Wooden stalls

Illuminated manuscript

MEDIEVAL RELICS

For Christians in the Middle Ages, relics became a symbol of religious truth. A relic might be a skeletal bone thought to have belonged to a very holy man or woman, or to a saint. Or, it may be an object, perhaps an article of clothing, believed to have belonged to people who figured in the Bible.

Raoul le Glabre, a monk who lived in France in the first half of the 11th century, described the strong attachment to relics, visible proof of God's presence on earth, that swept up the devout throughout medieval Europe. "Eight years after the thousandth year following the savior's birth [in 1008] . . . various clues led to the discovery of relics of saints in places where they had been hidden . . . the rumor about these discoveries led the faithful to come to these places . . . and it was not unusual to see the sick coming back cured, thanks to the intercession [aid] of the saints."

Christians began to pray in front of these relics so that the saints would ask God to

cure them. People, thousands of them, traveled from distant regions and even from other countries to witness these relics firsthand. These were the pilgrims.

When pilgrims—the sick, the lame, the blind, men and women and children—came upon the relics, some of them touched the stones of the church or cathedral where the relics were housed. Others prayed out loud or sang in a group directed by a monk. They approached the gold reliquaries, the heavily decorated boxes in the chapels that held the relics, and sunk to their knees in prayer.

Some of them sought relief from physical pain or a cure for an illness. Others came to be pardoned for a sin, a crime, or a serious mistake they had made. They left their families and homes to come and pray

to a saint or to beg Mary, the mother of Christ, whom they called Notre Dame (Our Lady), to accept their plea.

All cathedrals had relics. Whether they were authentic or not was not a question medieval people asked themselves. They believed that these remains from the land of Jesus could relieve their pain and soothe their conscience, help them get through

Reliquaries and shrines are containers to hold relics. They are made of gilded copper or silver and decorated with precious stones.

Reliquary of Saint Saturnin (Evreux)

The entire Sainte Chapelle, completed in only three years during the reign of Saint Louis, or Louis IX, was built as a reliquary to house a fragment from the "true cross" of Christ.

Welcoming the Pilgrims

The layout of a church or cathedral was designed to accommodate the many pilgrims who came to worship there. Should the lodging run by the monks be full, pilgrims slept in the side aisles. A special walkway around the choir allowed them to pass by the relics in the chapel.

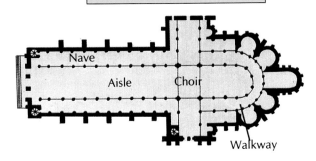

difficult times, and perhaps allow them to enter a better world when they died, where they could be close to God.

Some pilgrims traveled several days from a neighboring village to see a relic. Others traveled several months from a distant region or land. Some walked, while the wealthier ones rode on mules, donkeys, or horses. Pilgrims crisscrossed Europe at a pace of 15 to 20 miles (25 to 30 kilometers) a day.

Mont Saint Michel, Canterbury, Rome, Paris, Chartres, Jerusalem, and Santiago de Compostela welcomed thousands of pilgrims each year, as did hundreds of regional sanctuaries, or resting places.

NOTRE DAME

There is a story surrounding the construction of Notre Dame of Chartres that illustrates why so many medieval churches and cathedrals were called Notre Dame.

A city ravaged by fire was not an unusual occurrence in the Middle Ages. However, in 1194, when the cathedral in Chartres burned to the ground for the second time in fifty years, the townspeople were in despair.

This time, the cathedral was burned beyond repair. Everyone thought that the Virgin Mary had abandoned the faithful who gathered so often to pray to her. No one had the courage to rebuild Notre Dame of Chartres.

Then, one Sunday, the people of Chartres, who had gathered in front of the ruins of their cathedral, saw the bishop and monks approach in a procession. They carried a red shirt, a relic from the cathedral's crypt that had miraculously survived the fire. This precious article, believed to have belonged to the Virgin Mary, had been in the city's possession since the time of Charlemagne, in the 700s. Seeing it undamaged gave the people the faith they needed to build a new cathedral in which to house their relic.

A number of stories of this type were written during the Middle Ages. The central belief of the Christian Church (at this time, all Christians were Roman Catholic) was that the Virgin Mary was the mother of Jesus Christ, the son of God. Many medieval cities chose to put themselves under the protection of Mary.

Notre Dame in Amiens

Mary served as an intermediary, or a go-between, linking people to God. God was seen as distant and severe. Mary, who gave birth to God's son, was felt to be understanding and warm. From the 1100s on, most Christians prayed specifically to Mary to relieve their pain and to pardon their sins.

Virgin of the Nativity (Florence)

Our Lady appears in different forms in practically all medieval churches. Her name appears on buildings in cities all over Europe, including Florence in Italy; Fribourg, Lübeck, Strasbourg, and Treves in Germany; and Avignon and Dijon in France.

At Notre Dame of Paris, she decorates two of the doors. In Reims, she is the pier of its central entranceway. Notre Dame of Amiens is famous for its golden Virgin. And throughout Europe there are many statues, stained glass windows, and songs and hymns dedicated to Mary.

Ivory Virgin (1250)

Virgin and child (around 1330)

Virgin in vermilion, or bright red (1339)

A miniature of a knight who takes refuge in a church. His enemies kill him. A flame descends from the sky and burns his murderers. They will not be able to rise until they repent of their sin.

Offerings to Our Lady

Some 420 songs, 360 miracles (plays about the lives of the saints), 1,200 miniatures, and thousands of verses in honor of Mary were collected and then written down in an ancient book dedicated to the Virgin. The "Canticles of Saint Mary" were probably assembled or composed around 1250–1275 at the court of the Spanish king, Alphonse X. These are a history of the songs and images created to glorify Our Lady, by far the most celebrated heroine of the Middle Ages.

CELEBRATION IN THE CATHEDRAL

Many celebrations took place in the cathedral throughout the year, but there was one joyful holiday that a person would be lucky to celebrate once in a lifetime. This was the completion of the cathedral. It was a moment to be remembered, when all the years of work were over and the glorious new monument stood proudly in the center of the town.

No one missed the festivities. All of the monks and lords attended, as did the bishops from the neighboring towns. Each group of tradesmen gathered together under a special banner. The wealthy bourgeois came draped in fur. Everyone joined in the ceremony of placing the relics of the patron saint in their magnificent new home. The clerics broke into a Latin song. The procession moved out.

The crowd broke into applause as the priests in embroidered robes passed by, carrying the golden container that held the relics. The procession wound through all the main streets of the town. The sick, the lame, and the beggars jostled each other to approach the relics.

In the cathedral, the smell of incense wafted through the air. Candles made of beeswax illuminated the choir. Organ music and singing rose in harmony above the chattering of the crowd. Banners hung from the piers hiding the disorder of unfinished construction. Only the night before, the painters had filled in the last touches of blue and gold on the side entrance.

It was truly time to celebrate. The moment that everyone—all the cathedral builders, the townspeople, the peasants, the clergy, and the lords—had looked for-

ward to for as long as they could remember had finally arrived. Everyone was bursting with pride, gratitude, and awe at what they had done. They gave thanks to God and to one another for their cathedral.

All of the important events in life—birth, death, marriage, and initiation into knighthood—would be celebrated in the new cathedral. And each year, Easter (the celebration of the resurrection of Christ) and Christmas (the celebration of his birth) would be observed in the cathedral.

So, too, would other religious holidays, such as the Ascension (the celebration of Christ's rising to heaven forty days after his crucifixion), Pentecost (a feast on the seventh Sunday after Easter in remembrance of the Holy Spirit's coming to the apostles), and numerous saints' days throughout the year.

It was time to celebrate when a new bishop was named in the diocese. And it was time to celebrate when the king came to visit the town. Wooden arches covered with flowers made a canopy over the streets, and carpets of herbs were strewn on the ground. The cathedral overflowed with all the people from the town and the nearby lands craning their necks to catch a glimpse of the king. And everywhere, the cries of curious onlookers and excited children resounded through the streets.

Religious ceremonies began in the cathedral and rippled out into the square in front of the cathedral, and into the towns and villages around it.

On holidays, merchants set up their stalls. Butchers cut meat on portable tables, and fishmongers put their baskets of fish in the

shade. Drapers, secondhand clothes dealers, blacksmiths, and cobblers sold their wares to passersby. Monks preached in front of the cathedral. They staged mysteries and miracles, plays based on the Scriptures and the lives of the saints, hoping to catch the attention of the people watching the jugglers and bear tamers.

At carnival, or Mardi Gras, people made merry for days at a time before they settled down to fast and repent of their sins during Lent. Crowds of men and women ran into the streets in joyful celebration. This carnival, also known as the feast of crazy people or the innocent saints, wreaked havoc throughout the town.

The person who acted the craziest was named pope or bishop for the day. Some people put on monks' habits. Men dressed up like women or wore animal heads. People danced to country songs and ate and drank all they wanted. They sang and made fun of others, particularly the rich, the bourgeois, the clerics, and the lords. Everyone was boisterous. They even imitated the Latin sermons of the clerics, which many of the people could not understand.

Beyond the magnificence of their cathedrals and all the works of art inside them, medieval people passed on the traditions that originated in the beliefs behind the building of their cathedrals. And from their belief also came songs, music, and plays that we can still sing and hear and see today.

The Passion of Christ

On Easter Sunday, the most important holiday of the Christian faith, believers celebrated the resurrection, or rebirth, of Christ. Actors performed the story of Christ's life, called the Passion of Christ, on a colored platform in front of the church doors. The devils and demons enacting the Last Judgment frightened spectators or made them laugh. It was in these plays that the seeds of modern theater were sown.

THE LEGACY OF THE BUILDERS

Jean Deschamps was a cathedral builder. He was born in the 1100s, undoubtedly in Amiens. He was familiar with the new basilica in Saint Denis, Notre Dame in Paris, and several other cathedrals in the Île-de-France, a region in north central France. He directed the construction of the Clermont cathedral. Then he worked in Limoges, Rodez, and Narbonne. Later, other Deschamps, perhaps his sons, worked in Bordeaux, Toulouse, and even in Spain.

Thanks to masons and master builders such as Jean Deschamps, Gothic art, which was born in the fertile lands of the Île-de-France, spread throughout France and all the way to the distant reaches of Europe. In the time of the cathedrals, both people and ideas spread more quickly than might be imagined.

Belfry in Bruges, Belgium

Cloth market (Ieper, Belgium)

Students and pilgrims, monks, messengers of princes, merchants, and knights made their way along medieval roads and pathways. Cathedral builders were among these travelers. They moved from one construction site to another, perfecting their techniques. And in doing so, they ensured that the new art took hold.

Wherever the builders went, Gothic cathedrals rose up, as did abbeys and their cloisters, bridges, royal and papal palaces, town halls, belfries, great marketplaces, and grand Gothic houses.

Throughout the different regions in France and far beyond its borders, the Gothic cathedrals of Europe were constructed in the

Valentré Bridge
(Cahors, France)

Villard de Honnecourt

The cathedral builder Villard de Honnecourt is renowned today because his sketches, designs, and architectural plans have been passed down through the centuries. He was born near the end of the 12th century in the Cambrai region of northern France. He traveled as far afield as Hungary and brought back notebooks full of sketches. He drew the cathedrals of Chartres, Reims, Lausanne, Meaux, and Laon.

He also sketched some of the machines that were used at construction sites, including hydraulic saws and the jacks used to lift heavy loads. He was as interested in the laws of nature as he was in both sculpture and architecture. By explaining the rules of geometry and the art of making architectural plans and carving statues in his notebooks, Honnecourt hoped to help his readers, his fellow cathedral builders.

French style. The choir of the cathedral of Canterbury, for example, was built by a Frenchman named Guillaume of Sens. Anyone can see that the Bamberg cathedral in Germany bears a strong resemblance to the Laon cathedral in France, and that the Cologne cathedral is an imitation of the one in Amiens. In Spain, the cathedral of Toledo was built according to the same plan as that of Paris. And the Spanish cathedral in León resembles that of Reims.

Seven or eight hundred years ago, French cathedral builders traveled by foot from the Île-de-France to arrive in such distant cities as Prague in Czechoslovakia, Uppsala in Sweden, and Famagusta on the Mediterranean island of Cyprus to create their masterpiece—a cathedral.

These were the architects of the Middle Ages, and through their buildings we know them.

HOW TO EXPERIENCE A CATHEDRAL

To see a cathedral as it was between 1150 and 1350, you must first close your eyes. You must see it without the wood panels and tapestries, which were placed there in the 1500s and 1600s. You must imagine it without the large religious paintings, the gilded altars, and all the changes and new objects added over the centuries to bring the cathedral up to date.

ENTER THE CATHEDRAL

Instead of pews, imagine a crowd of men, women, and children. Ignore the silence. Listen to the voices from the Middle Ages. A group of merchants is meeting in an aisle; young monks keep repeating the same song in the choir; pilgrims inch toward the nave on their knees to honor the saints. A barking dog passes by, while a monk chases away two people who were playing dice under the shelter of the entranceway.

LOOK AROUND YOU

Notice the slender piers that rise toward the sky. In the Middle Ages, many of them were painted in lively colors. Walk over to the windows and study the panes of glass. If there is a raised platform along the wall, climb up to it and admire the windows from close up. Then, go back to the entranceway and take in the entire length of the nave at a single glance. After exploring the choir, stroll around the walkway until you come to the place where the transepts meet: you will be bathed in light.

GO OUTSIDE

Walk all around the building. Count your steps as a way to grasp the tremendous size of the monument. Look at the statues. Take in the kings, saints, and demons. Lift your head: strange birds and legendary beasts will seem on the verge of leaping from the stone. These are the gargoyles. Beneath the black and the dust of time, the Middle Ages are there.

CLIMB TO THE TOP

Finally, if it is permitted, climb to the heights. Experience the cathedral as a bird would, and don't forget to take in the flying buttresses and the city below. Pick out the old neighborhoods that surround it. You might even go down into the streets in search of medieval objects that retain traces of their past. The signs are there for those who know how to see.

Reims Cathedral

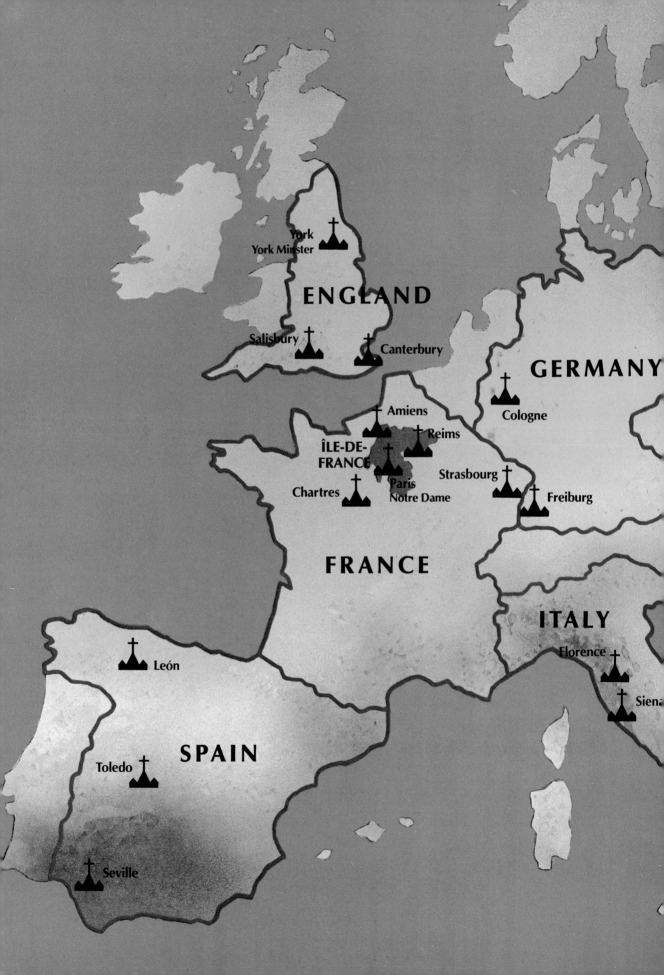

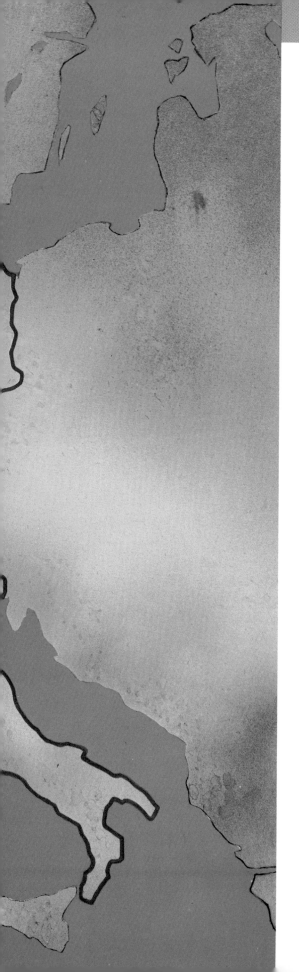

WHERE TO FIND A CATHEDRAL

ENGLAND

Canterbury Cathedral was an important pilgrimage site in the Middle Ages. Pilgrims went there to pray to the relics of Saint Thomas à Becket, an archbishop who was murdered in his own cathedral.

York Minster is the largest medieval cathedral in England. Its stained-glass windows are unusually beautiful.

Salisbury Cathedral has the highest tower built during the Middle Ages.

FRANCE

Notre Dame of Paris has very impressive flying buttresses. Its western rose window has the greatest amount of glass in relation to its supporting stone of any window made in the Middle Ages.

Chartres Cathedral is noted for its lovely stained glass, especially its blue glass, which is referred to as "Chartres blue." The two spires at its western end were built at different times and vary greatly in style.

Amiens Cathedral is considered by many to come closest to achieving the Gothic ideal. Although its vault soars to almost 140 feet (43 meters), people don't feel dwarfed by its great size. This is because the builders made sure that all its parts were in harmony with each other.

ITALY

Florence Cathedral, also called *Santa Maria del Fiore* or the *Duomo,* has a dome instead of a central tower. There are very few carvings on the outside walls. Because Italian builders had much beautiful stone available to them, they decorated the outside walls with sheets of many-colored marble laid in geometric patterns.

Siena Cathedral, also called the *Duomo*, is made of black and white stones laid in bands. High on its west wall are beautifully colored mosaics, which tell stories from the life of the Virgin Mary.

SPAIN

Seville Cathedral is a huge Gothic cathedral. During the late Middle Ages the Spanish were noted for their fine ironwork. Many beautiful wrought-iron screens from several different periods are found inside this cathedral.

Toledo Cathedral was the first Spanish cathedral to have a choir in the western part of the nave. This west choir became characteristic of later Spanish churches.

León Cathedral was built on the pilgrimage route to Santiago de Compostela. Its stained-glass windows are noted for their many yellow and gold colors. In a sunny country like Spain, these yellows and golds produce a strong, brilliant light inside.

GERMANY

Cologne Cathedral has the highest vault of any cathedral except for that of Beauvais Cathedral in France. This cathedral was also an important place for pilgrims. The bones of the Three Wise Men were thought to be in a reliquary here.

Fribourg Cathedral has a 377-foot (117-meter) spire. It looks very delicate in spite of its great height because of the elaborate tracery, or interlacing lines, carved into the stone.

Strasbourg Cathedral is now within the borders of France, but when it was built Strasbourg belonged to Germany. This church has an outstanding collection of medieval stained glass.

THE UNITED STATES

Since Europeans had not yet discovered America during the Middle Ages, there were no Gothic churches built in the United States. There are, however, Gothic Revival churches that imitate Gothic cathedrals. Because they were built much later—in the late nineteenth and twentieth centuries—builders used modern materials, such as steel and concrete, and the latest techniques and tools.

St. John the Divine in New York City was started in 1892 and remains unfinished today. Its vault is 125 feet (39 meters) high and when its two west towers are completed they will be 265 feet (82 meters) tall. Its central bronze portal was made by the same French firm that made the Statue of Liberty. Its spire will be higher than the spire of Salisbury Cathedral. The cathedral runs a training program to teach people how to carve stone.

St. Patrick's Cathedral in New York City sits right in the middle of the city, on Fifth Avenue. But where Gothic cathedrals were the tallest buildings in the Middle Ages, this church is dwarfed by the surrounding skyscrapers. Its Lady Chapel in the east end has an intense blue glass made specially for it at Chartres. St. Patrick's was under construction from 1850 until 1910.

Washington Cathedral, or *Episcopal Cathedral Church of St. Peter and St. Paul*, is in Washington, D.C. Its 301-foot (90-meter) bell tower rises from Mt. St. Alban, one of the highest hills in the District of Columbia. The stories carved in its stones are from the Creation, rather than from the life of the Virgin Mary. Because this church is new—it was started in 1907 and completed in 1990—you can see the brilliant effect medieval stained glass would have had when it was new.

DATES TO REMEMBER

1137 Louis VII becomes king of France.

1150 From this date on, cathedrals are under construction at Noyon, Senlis, Laon, Paris, and Soissons in France, and at Canterbury and Wells in England.

1152 Frederick Barbarossa becomes emperor of the Holy Roman Empire.

1179 Philip II (Philip Augustus) becomes king of England.

1189 Richard the Lionhearted becomes king of England.

1194 Chartres is rebuilt after a fire.

1195 From this day on, cathedrals are under construction and the new Gothic art is developing in the following places: Chartres, Bourges, Reims, Le Mans, Amiens, Beauvais, Strasbourg, Sainte Chapelle, Limoges, Rodez, Albi, and Paris in France; Bamberg, Limburg, Treves, and Cologne in Germany; León, Burgos, and Toledo in Spain; Siena and Florence in Italy; Utrecht in the Netherlands; Uppsala in Sweden; Famagusta in Cyprus.

1197 Richard the Lionhearted has the Château Gaillard constructed in France.

1226 Louis IX (Saint Louis) becomes king of France.

1235 Villard de Honnecourt writes a notebook for his students.

1297 Louis IX is made a saint by the pope.

1337 The Hundred Years' War between France and England begins.

FIND OUT MORE

Gandiol-Coppin, Brigitte. *Cathedrals: Stone Upon Stone*. Ossining, NY: Young Discovery Library, 1989.

Howarth, Sarah. *Medieval People*. Brookfield, CT: The Millbrook Press, 1992.

Howarth, Sarah. *Medieval Places*. Brookfield, CT: The Millbrook Press, 1992.

Macaulay, David. *Cathedral*. New York: Houghton Mifflin Co., 1981.

Macaulay, David. *Cathedral: The Story of Its Construction*. New York: Houghton Mifflin Co., 1973.

Watson, Percy. *Building the Medieval Cathedrals*. Minn., MN: Lerner Publishing, 1979.

GLOSSARY

Abbey. A monastery that is overseen by an abbot.

Apprentice. A person who is training to become a specialized artisan.

Artisan. Craftsman; a person who is trained in a skill such as woodwork, stonework, ironwork, or masonry.

Bishop. An important religious figure in the Catholic church who is in charge of a region, called a diocese. In medieval times, the bishop was the head of the cathedral.

Basilica. A large religious building modeled after Roman meeting halls.

Baptistry. A building where new believers and the newly born are baptised, or welcomed into the Christian faith.

Bourgeois. A person who belongs to the middle class; for example, a bourgeois shopkeeper.

Bourgeoisie. A term describing the middle class.

Canon. A special group of clergymen in charge of a cathedral's construction.

Cathedral. A church of a diocese. Most gothic cathedrals were built from around 1150 to 1350.

Centering. A collapsible wooden structure used to create a stone arch.

Chapel. A small place of worship; chapels date from the first century A.D.

Chapter. The name for the group of religious officials in charge of a cathedral's construction.

Clergy. The body of religious men who answer to the bishop.

Cleric. A member of the clergy.

Diocese. The region under the rule of a bishop.

Flying buttress. An exterior arch invented by gothic builders to balance against the outward pressure of an interior arch.

Gothic. A style of architecture that began in northern France and began to spread through western Europe during the 12th century.

Masonry. The craft of working with stone.

Master builder. The medieval equivalent of a modern-day architect. The person who planned and supervised the construction of a cathedral.

Medieval. A person or thing belonging to the Middle Ages.

Middle Ages. The period of European history from about 500 to about 1500.

Monastery. The residence of monks; includes a dormitory, dining hall, workshop, and cloister.

Mortar. The mixture of sand, lime, and water used to bind stones together in construction.

Monk. A member of the church who lives in a monastery.

Notre Dame. French for Our Lady. Refers to the Virgin Mary, a central figure in the Christian church.

Nave. The long, narrow central hall in a church.

Parish. A neighborhood church.

Passion. A play based on the story of Christ's life.

Pier. A slender column supporting the end of an arch.

Pilgrim. Someone who travels to see a relic.

Relic. A bone, object, or article of clothing believed to have belonged to a saint or highly religious person.

Reliquary. A decorated box in which a relic was placed. The cathedral was, in a sense, an enormous reliquary.

Ribbed vault. A lightweight vault coming to a point; invented by medieval builders.

Vault. An arched ceiling made of stone.

INDEX